COMPARABLE CAPTIONS

COMPARABLE CAPTIONS

Ken Keith Nakamura

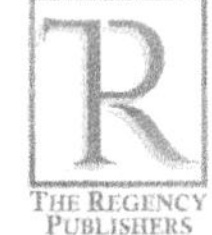

ISBN: 978-1-958517-21-5 (Paperback Edition)
ISBN: 978-1-958517-22-2 (Hardcover Edition)
ISBN: 978-1-958517-20-8 (E-book Edition)

Library of Congress Control Number: 2022911683

Book Ordering Information

The Regency Publishers, US
521 5th Ave 17th floor NY, NY10175
Phone Number: (315)537-3088 ext 1007
Email: info@theregencypublishers.com
www.theregencypublishers.com

Printed in the United States of America

Contents

BIOGRAPHY

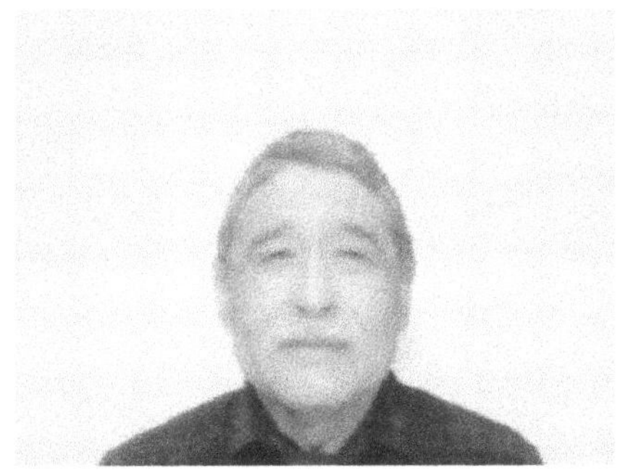

My name is Ken Keith Nakamura.

My collection of captions for the groundwork of Comparable Captions began in 1975.

I have a BA from York 1979 and have a Law Certificate in 1979 and 1980 from Centennial College, and a BED OTC from the University of Toronto in 1980-81. I've been a supply teacher in Toronto for 42 years, after 5 and 6 years of undergraduate and college education.

My brother and two sisters are teachers as are there husbands. I also have three children, twins, and a stepdaughter I haven't seen for over 22 years; all three are teachers and RCAF helicopter pilots.

THE PREAMBLE TO THE BOOK

The book can be made into a game like verbal Sudoku.

On each page, There is a blank space next to each caption where participants can write comments when they:

A. Make a debate using one of my captions
B. Act out on one or more of my captions
C. Respond to one or more of my captions
D. Make a speech using the captions
E. Create an essay about one of the captions
F. Create a pictograph picture from the caption
G. Make your own advertisement using your own prose or caption
H. Making a song out of the caption

The gander of geese and ducks their parkas and pillows in flight echoing their orders of the day

The Northern Cross of the Milky Way of factual illusions is not where are ancestors are

Encyclopedia judgements. The judicious fiddle. A litigious environment

Granite trees of autumn stand out like paint brushes and they say paint me paint me

Your Friends And Coworkers Are Like Chopsticks On The Accordion

Wooden fruit and vegetable insulation

Mellow colours and plasma breath

Curling ballet hockey

Communication Psychology. Philosophy appreciation

The dignity of electricity, essentialism, and delicious water

I benevolent you

Maple leaf paper and office marbles. It is written on stone. Temple tables

We are all cut from the same clothing

The shirt of the tundra and the skirt of the land the spread of the landscape

The might of recollection, elusive equity, and the good old days

Men bigger than their compact gear

The clouds groomed the hills

Evident Accountability transparent as Expo

Renovating comments

Magnificent vistas. The Dynasty of the Asylum

The vitamin cellar. The algorithms of a lottery

Qualitative and quantitative conjectures

Belief and relief

Inventory profits are high

The unknown good

The children's roundtable of moral quadratics. Luxurious Lego. The playdoh crusades

The script of the psyche and the hour of the subconscious

Bereavements privilege. An apology of thankfulness

Intermediate knowledge and character development

Taxes are investments

Governor of the citizen

The gravity of grammarians

We are a billion years away from the beginning of time. Who will we be in a billion years from now?

Synapse syntax. The liturgy of the ecosystem

Tuba band. No beans no means

Man and his committee of voices land on Mars as robot astronauts

A Guinness soft drink pop
Two-faced harmonica
Frustration and development
Keeping busy cheers you up

We are not beautiful hippopotamuses, we are gorgeous Rhinoceroses
The glory of cable
The speed bump of togetherness
Every delay has a consultation

Workaholic canoe. Admiral rowboat. The couch Pew
Great scholarship ends at the abyss
The humble humanitarian. A small window of longevity. The long term haul of becoming a better person. Making a useful difference
Spiritual cholesterol

The generosity of a genius
The novelty of goodwill
Beyond categorization
Squashed beef

Blanks of the rhyme
Wrens and seagulls
The leaning tower of responsibility and duty.
Italian architecture: A barbershop on every porch

TIN the number one conductor of high grade information.

The overwhelming workplace. Your work-load will increase, grow and become moderate

Dribble Dabble

Locomotion to location

Veterans and vetenarians an intersection of disciplines.

Artillery bowling rolling thunder

Contour mapping. Closest mm

Something is nothing and nothing is something

Renovating the healthcare institution

Hay beer

Dreams compromise loyalty

The Bear store

A Spiderman in every closet

Salary Celery

Shades of the paragraph

Aurora Borealis of the Galaxies

Duty Notes. Tailored made protocol
Arithmetic of Grammar. Mathematics of Language
Poetic Legislation
Faults are eroded by their strengths.

Eucharistic Euchre
A camera is a press release
The simplicity of excellence
Children are the movie stars of winter. They leave their footprints in the snow.

The hills were as grey as the sky as the snow lightened the day
A.M. Activists
PM'S Sandwich
Honourable patience

Winter personalities, colder than ethics
The tourists intelligensia
Meaningful and meaningless and the audi-tion of mindfulness
Bathtubs and chains

There's no KY-BOW in heaven
Right as paint
Hamsters jogging
Lemon Dishes two thumbs up

Chores of inspiration
Sorrow dispense evil
Muskie Muskeg
Piano of the log cabin

Fear embodies guilt and guilt embodies discipline
A baseball player's hand turned to leather.
Patient as a dentist
Semantics of Physics

Shear kilt
The proud banner of astronomy. The evening sky
The stars the police officers of the ghost of the Milky Way
Fruits of the labour movement. Optimism

The Clause of Integrity
Disclaimer a tribute
Man the amendment
Layman's Mayhem

Anonymous Maple Leaf sayings

Prose that does not leave a mark

Fussy Creativity

Defeat of Patriotism

Objectives are treasures

Crayons and the chipmunk

Nato singers

There's a caramelized trout at the end of a rainbow

Musical talk

Making a useful difference

A good question is a comment and or commentary and or open promise

Walk like a hike

Staggering author

Library juke box

The Dewey decimal point of publishing and broadcasting

Peanuts for potatoes

The grate Potato

The Beavers Igloo

Shopping for Utopia

The Haggis where you still taste the bagpipes

Our era has begun

The dessert sidewalks and windows of our great conurbane nation

Gopher Broke

Progress is an example of the Tabula Rasa

Redundant as a Xylophone
Mayors of Altruism
Maximum Empathy
The honest dollar

Snacking on economics
Cold and proud
Trail to the room
Honor Humor

Language is impressive
Man is the partner of the creator
Icicles and manners
The pause between God and man

A poor man's snowman on a millionaire's toboggan

Scrooge Writers

Razor blade hockey and skating

The umbrella fell and elastic geometry

Humorous Chromosome

Brave brain

Odyssey of snow. Canuck Snowflakes

The epiphany of the symphony

Canada the land of ice and snow where the ancient winds blow
and the rain is a white as snow

Spud fish. A halibut of a potato

Rain makes you stronger

Giraffe graphing

A clean mark
You grow like a graph
Rivera ravine look
Yoga Yogurt

Inflation of the balloon
Further than farther
Cheerleading politics.
The Political schoolhouse

Bongo Command
Bleachers of the lecture
Better half of the plate
Clean manure

Lackadaisical lactose
Oscar KABOSA
Glide calories
Raining like God's pee

Yellow memoirs turning gold
Serious silly clock
Our product is job satisfaction
The engine of the journal

Jingle jungle
The honor roll of attendance
Eventually ethical
Heart like a gear

Cliff hanger coat hanger
Mug warming cafe
Shotgun of the bong
Cooking like coaching

Meal presentation is everything next to hunger
Whistling ravens
The question of privilege and fairness
Risks and Benefits
Loafing around the flour mill

Puck eclipse
Chalkboard Mandate
Commissioner of pins and buttons.
Mushrooming of human rights

Proud metal

Ties as fatigues

Jealous pimples

Love creates art and art creates an image that is a representative or representation of reality

Amber red and green. Patterns of successful themes

Natural teachings

Success is measured by effort

Appearance of brilliance

Tales of wildlife

Poetic medication that footnotes the world

Fictional confessions

Balance the budget of materialism. Start responsive spending

Your hands are nude
Legal acts of literature
Work as a savings
Survival with momentum

The welfare of fraud in Providence
Watermelon fountain
The reincarnated voice. The stomachs paramecium gland
Daily tribulations and joy clues of the good afterlife

Close as a cigar
Thinking around the circle a sings-song
Spoon then the shovel
A carefree explique on cleaning

The malice of a mallard.
Motown hood
Acceptable respectable and approved

Utterance extinction
Info guns
Labs to restaurants
Good deeds that multiply

Dinosaur teeth and gypsy feet
Good schooling is like a regiment without a rank
Industrial recreation and the Kleenex of sports
Remembrance of the cattle axe

Glacial pyramids of our governing bodies

The human mind of transit. The awe of travel

Thick plate

Paper chefs. The more you clean the more you cook a clean plate means dessert

Cookie pills

Serenade of salutations

The countless victories of solidarity .

All-star activities

Bagel Sunday born again steaks

Hurdle the turtle

River Applause

The children and the community are the home grown peacekeepers of our great nation

Advertising. The Evolution of the syllogism.

Powerful comfortable prayers make for a comfortable conscience.

The Innocence of loss. Elusive equity

Halitosis mitosis. Onion visine

School is like a book that never closes

Bambi archery

Church and the garage

Hockey night in Hollywood

Snow clouds are where the winter galaxies are.

Speechmaker making a bag of goodies in a time of crisis.

Science and pollution

Puzzle of confusion manifestations of manifestos

The failure of writing and the success of a man

Institutions are man made mountains

The city is my country home

The gifted spotlight of exceptional students

The love of work. Working is fun

Instant lamb stew

Vulnerability of humanity

The Democracy of television

Make a light bulb using mirrors

Content makes its own message

Winter personalities and ethics.

Good broadcasting and Journalism is like a good medium steak

Nuclear family Pluto Plutonium Uranus Uranium and Mercury Pressure

Faith Swimming

Colonel clerk. The general secret

Anthem prayer

Humidity perseverance.

Sustenance in Appetite

The depression of ambition

Latent compliments

Granny Smith Smiley faces

Grinning grapefruit breakfast

The vinegar bouquet of the wine

Navy nose. Faster than mistakes and slower than the flow

Landscape Architects the bridge home

The moon is as white as a snowball a soccer ball a golf ball a baseball a ping pong ball

Newtonian balls. Ballpoint swords

Cranberries. Giving thanks everyday

Electrifying the airplane and aerospace industry

Factory funny and warehouse flue

Make something equitable

Gondola with the wind

Windy the sailor's girlfriend

Popular as a sailor

Mouse of the moose

Elaine the bowler's girlfriend. Canon ball bowling without the fodder

Adequate improvement of the intellect
Einstein and Aristotle are students of modern man
Prisoner of history Recycling plant
The earth is the center of the big bang

Anchor of geography
Skinny milk
Bow to the arrow
Alphabet accountants

Our flag salutes our children when they are at ease
Don't choke on the artichoke.
The Bayonet knife of gastronomy
Tears of the stomach

The editors of the bar.
The late early edition of the party conversation
The Pony Express
The Corny Meadow

The audience is your friend
Biking like shinny hockey
Success of worrying
Jet to cave

Proud animals wait
Celibacy is a desire
Certified fulfillment
Steps of the next decade

Caricature of juxtapositions
The nib of metaphysics touching the first metaphor
Bomb every city with amended legislation
Presbyterian like pedestrians

Stable Fame.
Training For Goodness .
Prolific beaches. Jazz poetry in the subtle breeze.
Seamless knowledge is acknowledgement.
Conjuring up conjugations

The confident Laureate directing leadership
Epistemology, pedagogy and curriculum.
Prose that does not leave a mark.
Tracing the landscape
Threw the snowball effect

Fight at doing your job right

Beefing up the poems

A foreign tomorrow

The cosmos comet of gender sensitivity and cursive writing

Merit race the face of the race

A whale tomorrow

Elucidated carbon

There enough salad to feed an army of Canada's moose

The Co-efficient of context

Critique improvements and consistency

The power of the sword and expensive prosperity

Indoor rain outdoor characters

Pilgrim saturations
Social justice diversification
Praise the food
Banjo wife

Deaf apologies
The need to assess. Committees and communion
Negotiating nursery rhymes and the inequities in your daily contract
Naturally tasteless you're a cliché

The web of free will
Redressing in the shadows
Proper numbers behave. Improper slurring numbers misbehave
Bourgeoisie cheese

Snoring a teardrop
Fairness of literature
Testament of the fridge
A strikes decimal point

Minutes of the revolution
The veil of the treble clef
Freedom in stress
Emotive language is the roots of our laws

White light of dentine
You're a giant to your childhood
Ornaments of religions
Dethroning a regime every May

Developing a criminals conscience to his demise

An excellent attitude is an achievement

Therapy writing

Folks of the union spokes

Your words are on fire

Oink Goes The Eraser And Moo Goes The Resources.

Tip of the ice cube

Preservation and conservation a natural motive

Noble flexibility

When your river is down and out

Epigrams that exonerate you

Thunder over the puddle

Nature's fascism
Salute your hands-on organization
Urban isolation
Labor arrived at the door of bureaucracy

We are above the water and the land
The guns of the free world unite
Solitude the hands of the clock away
The expert of existence and essentialism

Cowboys and popcorn
Guns are junk built by the museum
Scribble talking
Healthy habits

Barbecue clouds
Legal bells erasing wonder
The indescribable sky
A classroom is an ethical stimulus

Logic grammar
Canadian fire
Church building. The woodworker's sermon
Manifest graffiti

Canadian Nationalism. The drummer is idle
Sap Engineering
Boasting and overeating. Eat responsibly
The chromatic choir. The gravy forged the grovey. Fussy creativity

Revival. Vitalization of man-animal and machine and music

The rivalry team

Limousine politicians

Rubrics ease

The happy ruler. Troubleshooting that does not cost money

Put a muffler on your diatribe

Open and closed reading

Stay tuned for comic identification

Pragmatically tired

Myths of the legends. Rural and urban

Natural and artificial

Perceived products

We respect in, indifference and in reservation
Philosophical breakthroughs
Touch electricity
Respect in neutrality. Truck drivers

The failure of capitalism and the advent of breakfast
Sapphire toothpaste and fluoride bubble gum
Pyramid of memory
Altos of the workplace

Factor actor
A good meal is like a pill of good health
Oracle of the edible
The friendship of Independence

Terminal grazing
To a point Arrogance breeds equality
Waiting in the line of the nation's builders,
Nasal Damsel

Alkaline names are used to make a better world
Play on the going and the waiting
The cattle's military academy
The Pronoun I and Number 1

The glucose girl
Shark tuna sandwich
The Prairie lakes blow up and rumble
Rank philanthropy

The Cadillac castles of the neighborhood

What the international chair said to the global pupils your desk is the best

Bowing Protestants and Catholics

Mom and Dad are giants

A cows soldier a whale of hardships

Perfect behavior inspires

Teaching is an innovation and an Activity

Prose establishes corporations

Cheers to the archetypes of intertainment and industry.

Lending a helping hand

Solitaire cookie

Reality over fiction. Confessions

Arbitrations victorious window

The Constitution of linguistics
8 billion ghosts
Winter weather is a polar bear fridge
The bell curve of sergeant's computer

Perfume sausages
Paint yourself into the boat
Speechless for a remedy
Property hooks

Less is more
Doodling economists
The PR of recess
The concept is when ideas become ideology. Forest fire prevention. Take an off the shelf telescope. Equip it with an adade and asquith computer and aim it at the earth instead of the galaxies. That will detect fires to the nearest fentogram

The property of best practices
The moment was a gigantic flounder
The paradise garden. The agricultural industry
Tangible gifts.

Baptize the boat
Bullet of contraband
The compass of good news
Photon photos

The Plumber's throne
The pennys ink blot
Your week as an astronaut
Beware of the watchdog of 2080
The magnificence of Algonquin and the pyramids

Private-public PUB guidelines
Group hierarchy. The invitation of your personal prospectus
Intermediate mentoring. Grade a resolutions
Speed up comprehensions

The best den and harp
Fluoride ice cream.
Pronunciations, prerogative pierogies
The mosque in bloom

The frogs' ribbiting was righteous
Sleeping imitates playing
Smiling statues
The effectiveness of careers. Networking

Laugh, it's uphill

Rameses' cat Lancelot

Your works compliment you

The duration of imposition and the disposition of influence

Data prices Value

Endeavours over the commonplace. Mundane importance.

Spelling dictators

The resume grows

The broom of the room

Guilty tummy

Stockyard DNA

The parameters of dynamics. Neopolitan microphones. Beyond every book a song. The windpipe flute

A good sextant is good health
The elders of the community stand out like Alders
Tomorrow is as long as yesterday was a briefing
Scripture and sanctimony makes for excitement

Stewardships and members verbatim matters. Your 6th senses and your 7 th textbook
Happy fast forward
The gavel of sign language
The singing paint brush

Turkey Angels. A nickel for wawa
The gold bullion tribute to the vast outdoors. The miracle of culture
The paradigms and consumerism of happiness
A hula hoop down time selfie

Benevolence. When we give something away that we don't have. Shopping for utopia and the tangible gifts of empowerment. Buddha gave his wife cultured pearls. And his wife gave the world the first rosary.

The labyrinth of your lexicography. In your daily diction of splendor and rhetoric of suppression and sovereignty

Ammo food

The bay of funding

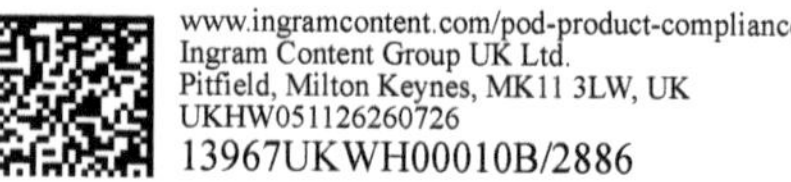
www.ingramcontent.com/pod-product-compliance
Ingram Content Group UK Ltd.
Pitfield, Milton Keynes, MK11 3LW, UK
UKHW051126260726
13967UKWH00010B/2886

9 781958 517215